Pirates of Devon & Cornwall

Richard Peirce

Published by:
Shark Cornwall, Dulverton House, Crooklets,
Bude, Cornwall, EX23 8NE.

First published March 2010
Second printing May 2010
Third printing June 2011

ISBN no. 978-0-9558694-1-9

Photographs: Richard Peirce
Design and Artwork: Anthony Moulton
Printed and bound in England by
SR Print Management Limited, Watling Court, Orbital Plaza,
Cannock, Staffordshire. WS11 0EL

– – – – – –

SOON TO BE PUBLISHED BY THE SAME AUTHOR
"Shark adventures – the expeditions"
"Pocket guide to Sharks in British Seas"
"Sharks in British Seas" (second edition)

OTHER PRODUCTS
"Sharks in British Seas" - Book (Richard Peirce)
"Sharks in British Seas" - DVD (Simon Spear - Richard Peirce)
"Sharks off Cornwall and Devon" - Book (Tor Mark Publishing)
"Shark Attack Britain" - DVD (Shark Bay Films end 2010)

All books and DVD's can be bought through our website
www.sharkconsoc.com

Pirates of Devon & Cornwall

'Pirate' is a word that has stirred the blood and struck fear into the hearts of men for hundreds of years. These maritime thieves have plundered, murdered, raped and pillaged in all the world's seas, yet they also have a romantic image. I suspect the best known pirate today is the fictional Captain Jack Sparrow from the 'Pirates of the Caribbean' films. Say pirate and the face that will come to most minds is that of the film's lovable off the wall rogue played by Johnny Depp.

Captain Jack Rackham, who probably inspired the character played by Depp, was also known as Calico Jack because of his fondness for colourful clothing. Calico Jack may have been a likeable, womanising rogue, but many pirates were full-on murdering cut-throats and the romantic image pirates have gained through Hollywood is not a true reflection of the facts.

Devon and Cornwall were home to many of Britain's pirates and this short book looks at them and seeks to separate the fact from the fiction. While I have concentrated on pirates from the two counties I have not ignored others who were born outside their borders. To look at the golden age of piracy without mentioning Edward Teach (Blackbeard) from Bristol would be a glaring omission; equally it would be wrong to leave out such a significant figure as William Dampier because he was born a few miles inside Somerset. Pirates may not have been romantic heroes, but they were a colourful bunch who often made history and I hope you enjoy meeting them.

This book is dedicated to my wonderful wife
Jacqui, with whom I have shared many
adventures, and who must at times have
wondered whether she was married to
someone who would have been happier
living in yesterday's world. Her love, support,
forbearance and patience have enabled me
to live many of my dreams.

Richard

Pirates of
Devon & Cornwall

Chapter One

The First Pirates

Who were the first pirates? The answer depends on how the word is defined. Saxon warrior pirates terrorized sailors in northern Europe's coastal waters but little is known of them. Using some definitions, the Vikings were perhaps northern Europe's first pirates, but I consider them more as raiders (and sometimes invaders), than pirates. Certainly looting, rape and pillage were all activities the Vikings excelled at, but most of the time they returned home after the raids.

Sometimes Viking forces were large and 'invader' rather than 'raider' is certainly the right term. In 836 a substantial force of thirty-five ships landed at Carhampton in Somerset and defeated the Saxon King Egbert of Wessex. In 838 a major Viking force joined with the Cornish and again fought King Egbert, but this time the Saxon king won the day.

The Viking raids and invasions continued through the 800s and by 871 the Norsemen were locked in battle against the new king of Wessex – Alfred the Great. In 878 Alfred won a decisive battle against the Vikings at Ethandum which is thought to be in what is now Wiltshire. The Viking wars then moved east, and while some seafaring sons of Devon and Cornwall turned their hands to piracy, there is little record.

In 1135 King Henry gave Lundy Island to Jourdan de Marisco. The de Mariscos had arrived in England with William the Conqueror and were a rough clan of brigands who turned Lundy Island into a pirate refuge as time went on.

There was only one safe place to land on the island, and the de Mariscos added their own fortifications to those provided by nature. Racing tides, dangerous rocks and high cliffs all make Lundy a treacherous place, and all but impregnable to invaders. In 1160 Jourdan de Marisco lost Lundy when the King gave the island to the Knights Templar. However he refused to leave and denied entry to the knights, and so as a compensation they were granted the income from the de Marisco estates in Somerset.

The de Mariscos still held Lundy in the first half of the thirteenth century when Sir William de Marisco started to use the island as a base for pirate operations. Marisco Castle on Lundy was built for defence and even had catapults deployed to repel invaders. Sir William's pirate fleet operated in the Bristol Channel, up into the Irish Sea and out into the Atlantic. He carried on his piracy almost with impunity, knowing he had a safe refuge to retreat to in case of need. Later he realised that kidnapping was a much easier way to make profits, and he took to kidnapping rich merchants and holding them at Marisco Castle until their ransoms were paid.

Sir William did not get on well with King Henry III and was involved in a plot to kill him. The assassination attempt failed, and Sir William fled to his pirate lair. The King's men were able one night to make a surprise landing and captured Sir William and sixteen of his men. They were found guilty of treason and Sir William gained the notoriety of being the first man to be hung drawn and quartered – it is said that this punishment was devised specially for him. He was hanged, his genitals severed, and his stomach and intestines were removed and were burned in front of him. His other organs were also taken out and his head cut off before his body was quartered and displayed at prominent places around London. Using the generally accepted definition of a pirate I believe Sir William was probably among Britain's first. He was certainly notorious and his death was a bloody end to a roguish career.

The outbreak of the Hundred Years War in 1337 meant that many of the great landowners and other leading figures were away for long periods fighting the French. This left parts of Britain without governing authority which gave criminals many opportunities. North Cornwall was as lawless as anywhere, and a gang of pirates based at Widemouth Bay preyed on passing small vessels.

In 1342 the *La Trinite* of Fowey anchored in the bay was boarded and looted by a local gang, the ship then washed ashore and broke up. Coincidentally in 1346 another vessel of the same name carrying wines and other goods from Bordeaux to Bristol, was also seized off Widemouth and her cargo stolen.

William de St. Gennys, Nicholas de Bere and John, Nicholas and Reginald Penfound were all among the accused.

In 1357 William Penfound of Penfound Manor was a curate of St Winwaloe Church in Poundstock. Legend has it that he was also a leading member of the local pirate gang, and on December 27th 1357 a group of armed men burst into the church at the end of the service and murdered Penfound at the altar. Other Penfounds were wounded in the fighting and in February 1358 King Edward ordered the arrest of the culprits. The Bevilles of Woolston Manor were central to the murder, but many other local families were clearly also involved. They were the same families which were involved in piracy along Cornwall's north coast. Was the murder a family feud, or a falling out among pirates? We will never know but although tried and acknowledged as guilty no one was hanged for the murder. William Penfound is said to haunt the church to this day, so perhaps he is still seeking justice for his murder.

Defining piracy in these times gone by can be a difficult exercise because the lines between legitimacy and illegitimacy are often blurred. Merchant ships were sometimes called upon for defence and constituted a navy of sorts. They could attack enemies of the crown with impunity and commonly decided that foreign and enemy were the same thing. The court in London was a long way from remote West Country ports and captains would not always know who England was fighting.

For West of England pirates the Hundred Years War period was a time of great opportunity. John Hawley was the mayor of Dartmouth and an eminently respected senior pillar of the community. In 1399 he led an attack on a French fleet and captured thirty-four ships which he brought back to Dartmouth. The residents of the town joined in the victory celebrations as they helped drink the 1500 tonnes of wine that had been aboard the French ships. John Hawley died in 1408 and his son of the same name carried on the family piracy business. Dartmouth was a pirate town and a significant part of the town's income came from looting and piracy. Raiders from Dartmouth harassed the French mercilessly and in 1404 the French retaliated by trying to take the town. Hawley's sea defences were formidable and so the French landed nearby at Slapton, hoping to take Dartmouth by land. They were met by Hawley leading a motley force made up of levies, militia, and townsfolk. The Dartmouth pirates won the day and virtually the entire French force was killed or captured.

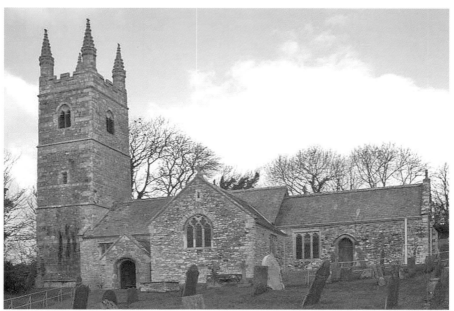

Poundstock church where William Penfound was murdered

Penfound Coat of Arms in Poundstock church

Cornwall's Fowey was a pirate town which rivalled Dartmouth. Fowey had been a significant sea port in the thirteenth and fourteenth centuries but had declined. By the early fifteenth century Fowey was a major centre for pirates. Mark Mixtow was a Fowey pirate, and Sir Hugh Courteney and Thomas Bodulgate were also Cornish pirates of the same period. Leading families like the Trevelyans and the Arundells had pirates among their members.

By the end of the century America had been discovered and the British navy of King Henry VIII not only curtailed pirate operations but also offered 'legal' employment for seamen.

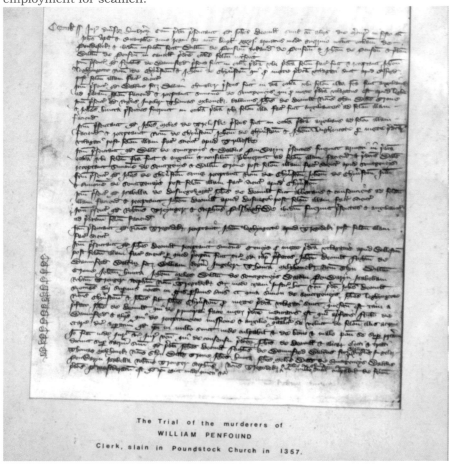

The Trial of the murderers of
WILLIAM PENFOUND
Clerk, slain in Poundstock Church in 1357.

Document in Latin recording the trial of the murderers of William Penfound (Poundstock church)

6

Chapter Two

The Elizabethans/Sir Francis Drake

Sir Richard Rogers of Bryanston owned the land both to the west and east of Lulworth Cove in Dorset. This gave him a private harbour and in the middle of Elizabeth I's reign Lulworth Cove was a centre for piracy. Sir Richard and his brother Francis operated Lulworth as a private fiefdom and a refuge for pirates, but they fell foul of the Crown and by 1580 Studland Bay to the east of Lulworth had become the West of England's centre for piracy. By a quirk of the law Studland Bay lay beyond the control of the Admiralty and pirates from Devon and Cornwall, Wales, Ireland, and Holland came there for refuge and to trade their ill-gotten gains.

One of the greatest figures of the Studland pirate era was John Piers of Padstow. He had started his pirate career working along his own native north Cornish coast from Padstow to Hartland, out to Lundy and into the Bristol channel. Piers soon spread his wings and his area of operations stretched the length of the English Channel from the eastern end to the Atlantic and into the Irish Sea. He was an audacious man who regularly plundered Royal Navy ships and once blockaded Rye harbour in Sussex. In Padstow he was something of a Robin Hood hero figure, and his mother was a major trader of her son's plundered goods. She had a reputation as a witch which guaranteed security for herself, and their merchandise. However in 1581 Piers and his crew were arrested, and taken to Corfe Castle where they were tried and found guilty. They were hanged overlooking the bay.

Studland may have been the major pirate centre of the 1570's and early 1580's, but the Devon pirates were still working out of Dartmouth and using Torbay's natural anchorage as a shelter area. Captains Prideaux and Clarke were notable among south Devon's pirates of the time, while in Cornwall the Killigrew family had a direct involvement with piracy. The Killigrews were one of the most successful and powerful families in Westcountry pirate history, and were probably the leading Cornish pirates of all time. They owned a piece of ground at Pendennis strategically placed to look out over Falmouth Harbour. King Henry VIII not only paid Sir John Killigrew a rent for the land, but also made him captain of the castle that was sited there. During Queen Elizabeth's reign the castle was enlarged and the Killigrews virtually controlled Falmouth harbour and its approaches. The main family residence was at Arwenack House which still stands today and which was used as a store for a huge range of stolen goods.

The ships of the first Sir John Killigrew openly indulged in piracy and operated all around the English Channel, the north-east Atlantic, and the Celtic and Irish seas. For three generations successive Sir John Killigrews were involved in piracy, although it was the first Sir John who died in 1597 who was the most active. By the time of the death of the third Sir John the family profited from piracy in only a relatively small way.

Being an active pirate is one thing, but being in authority and turning a blind eye to the acts of others would make you just as guilty in modern times. The Killigrews financed and supplied many others and took a share of the spoils. We will soon see how the Queen was a shareholder in Drake's 'merchant voyages', and this example was followed throughout the governing establishment. Gilbert Peppit, the Sergeant of the Devon Admiralty Court, was arrested for his dealings with Devon pirates. At the same time it was rumoured that the Mayor of Exeter had close pirate connections, and Sir John Humphrey looted ships in Dartmouth and Torbay. The head of the Cornish Commission for piracy in 1577 was none other than Sir John Killigrew!

While piracy was mainly the occupation of men, their women-folk often got involved. We saw earlier how the mother of John Piers of Padstow was involved in her son's pirate acts. In the Killigrew family the wives of all three Sir John Killigrews were involved in their husband's business activities. Elizabeth was the wife of the first Sir John and mother of the second. Some speculate that Lady Elizabeth Killigrew may have been the inspiration for Lady Dona St Columb in Daphne du Maurier's 'Frenchmans Creek'. It was Lady Elizabeth who organised the rifling of a Spanish vessel which bad weather had forced into Falmouth harbour. The *Marie* was rumoured to be carrying a fortune and when the rumours reached Killigrew ears the temptation proved too much and a raiding party was ferried out to her aboard Sir John's own pinnace. (Pinnaces were light, shallow-draft craft that were fast and

Padstow harbour in October 2009, the same harbour which the pirate John Piers operated from in the 1500's

Killigrew monument outside Arwenack House, Falmouth

Killigrew family Coat of Arms found outside Arwenack House, Falmouth

manoeuvrable) The subsequent investigation into this act of piracy was limited, perhaps due to Sir John being the head of the Cornish Commission for Piracy! However action was eventually taken and two Killigrew family servants, John Hawkins and Henry Kendall, were found guilty of the crime. The rumours of treasure had proved to be exaggerated, but the *Marie* was carrying some fine bolts of cloth which were divided among the Killigrews and those who carried out the raid.

One of the pirate captains the Killigrews did business with was Robert Hicks. Hicks is known to have associated with many of the West of England's pirate captains. He was adept at seizing ships and took Spanish, Dutch and Danish vessels. He was captured in late 1577 and hanged in early 1578.

––––––––––

Among the best known names of the Elizabethan era are those of Drake, Raleigh, Grenville and Hawkins. They are known as explorers, adventurers and merchant sailors, but the line between piracy and legitimate maritime activity was often blurred, and some of the time they may have been on the wrong side of this line.

Queen Elizabeth referred to Sir Francis Drake as 'her pirate' and while there is no doubt of Drake's patriotism and his devotion to his Queen, there is also little doubt that the Queen's description was accurate. Drake was a true son of Devon and was born about 1542 at Crowndale near Tavistock. He was a cousin of the well known Hawkins family of Plymouth who were established merchants and slavers. Drake's career as a seaman began in the late 1550's when he took employment in a junior capacity on a coastal vessel. In 1563 he sailed as a junior officer on a Hawkins trading voyage to Africa.

During the next few years he sailed on many Hawkins expeditions. By 1568 Drake had command of the *Judith* and sailed as part of a squadron on a slaving voyage. Slaves were captured in Africa and transported to the Spanish colonies in the New World for sale. Hawkins was a well-established figure in this ghastly trade and the Spanish were eager customers.

Hawkins and Drake made a few such voyages during this period, and although the Spaniards were technically forbidden to trade with merchants from other nations, the business was conducted without confrontation most of the time. At the end of the third voyage Hawkins was trading at Borburata on the mainland and he sent Drake ahead to Rio de la Hacha to reconnoitre. On arrival Drake was fired on by the town's Spanish garrison and when Hawkins arrived they landed and took the town.

Main building Pendennis Castle, Falmouth

ARWENACK

Arms of the Arwenack family.

Arwenack about 1545, from Henry VIII's Great Map.

Arwenack about 1670, from a map in the County Record Office.

Arwenack is the oldest example of domestic architecture in Falmouth. Originally owned by a family of the same name, it came to the Killigrews by marriage about 1385. Fragments of the 14th century house remain, but the form of Arwenack as we see it today appears to have been established in the mid-16th century by John Killigrew, the first Governor of Pendennis Castle.

Successive Killigrews enlarged and modified the house until it was overtaken by disaster during the Civil War. How much of Arwenack was actually destroyed is still open to question, but it seems that little or no new building took place on the site until the late 18th century. At this date wings flanking the courtyard were doubled, and the house assumed more or less its present day appearance.

By 1978 Arwenack was in poor structural condition, and but for the intervention of the Redruth builders Percy Williams & Sons Ltd. might have been lost to Falmouth. It has now been extensively repaired and converted into several dwellings.

Arwenack is Cornish for *on the marshy place*, doubtless an apt description of the original house before the development of Falmouth under the influence of the Killigrew family.

Sign erected by Falmouth Civic Society with the aid of a Heritage Interpretation Grant from the Carnegie United Kingdom Trust.

Arms of the Killigrew family.

Arwenack about 1570, from Lord Burghley's atlas.

Arwenack in 1773, from a map in the Public Library.

Plaque outside Arwenack House, Falmouth

Pendennis Castle, Falmouth

Pendennis Castle commands the approaches to Falmouth occupying a key coastal position

After taking the town, Hawkins and Drake used their position of strength to complete various trading activities, including selling eighty slaves, cloth and other goods. They then decided to head for home and the small fleet was caught in a storm off Florida on the way home and was badly battered. They were forced to run for the larger Spanish port of San Juan de Ulua for shelter and to conduct repairs. Shortly after their arrival the treasure fleet arrived from Spain on its annual expedition to collect the produce from the mines in Mexico. Hawkins and Drake were confronted by thirteen heavily armed galleons. There was a stand off, Hawkins was blocking the entrance to the harbour and risked a major incident if he didn't let the Spanish enter. On the other hand he was fearful of being in a weak position if he let them in and was then attacked. The Spanish commander couldn't wait outside and risk the weather in unsheltered waters, nor could he fight his way in. They negotiated and Hawkins let the Spanish in on the understanding there would be no subsequent attack. Three days after entering the harbour the Spanish broke their word. Many of Hawkins and Drake's men were ashore at the time and were slaughtered as they tried to reach their ships. The *Judith*, the *Minion* and the *Jesus* managed to escape but were fired on as they made for the open sea. The *Jesus* had all her masts shot through and was used as a shield by the *Minion* as Hawkins made his escape. Hawkins made for the Mexican coast where 100 of his men asked to be put ashore. Only twenty of the *Minion* crew made it home to England. Drake had made straight for England with the *Judith* and arrived safely. According to Hawkins, Drake abandoned him, however this did not appear to affect their future relationship so it appears that Hawkins forgave him. There is little doubt that the battle of San Juan de Ulua changed history, in that the Spanish double cross would never be forgotten by Drake who justified his next fifteen years of outright piracy against the Spanish by drawing on his righteous and religious indignation.

The Isthmus of Panama leads on to the north coast of South America which is the mainland southern rim of the Caribbean sea. This was the Spanish Main and the focus of Drake's attentions when he set sail in 1570 aboard the tiny twenty five ton *Swan*. On this voyage Drake discovered a small natural harbour he named Port Pheasant which was well protected from the sea and easily defensible against enemies. He also reconnoitered Nombre de Dios which was one of the principal treasure ports of the Spanish Main. Twice a year Spanish galleons anchored in the bay and loaded gold and silver mined in Peru and Bolivia. Nombre de Dios had no fine buildings like Cartagena and Panama, it was a shanty town of some two hundred houses and sheds.

He returned to England and then in May 1572 he departed from Plymouth on a new voyage with two vessels, the *Pasco* and the *Swan*, the latter commanded by his brother John. Forty-nine days later they sailed back into Port Pheasant. Drake and his crew had thought the existence of Port Pheasant was their secret, but on stepping ashore he found a message on a lead plate nailed to a tree. It was a warning from John Garret who was another Devonian and a friend of Drake's. Garret warned that the Spaniards were aware of Port Pheasant and indeed had stolen some spare supplies and equipment that Drake had left buried there on his last visit.

The discovery that his base was known to the Spanish did not deter him and he set about fortifying Port Pheasant against their return, and assembled the three pinnaces they had brought with them in their holds.

Drake's plan was to use Port Pheasant as a safe base for his raiding operations against the Spanish, starting with a raid on the treasure town of Nombre de Dios. While preparations were underway another English captain called James Raunse sailed into Port Pheasant. Clearly Drake's secret port was not such a secret after all! The *Pasco* and the *Swan* carried a total of seventy-three men, and Drake had also been joined by escaped slaves called Cimarroons who lived in the jungle and hated the Spanish. He now asked Captain Raunse to join them for the raid on Nombre de Dios.

In July with a small force of only around sixty men they reached the town at 3.00 a.m. and made for the shore battery of six guns. The one man guarding the guns fled, and Drake split his small force in two. He commanded one and the other was led by his brother John and one of the officers, John Oxenham. Drake led his force of forty into town from the east beating drums and sounding trumpets. The inhabitants thought they were being attacked by a large group, panicked and ran. There was however a small party of fourteen or fifteen who armed themselves with muskets and met Drake's force in the market square. A volley was fired and Drake's trumpeter was killed and Drake shot in the leg.

John Drake and John Oxenham then attacked the Spaniards from behind and they were either killed, captured, or escaped. Drake led his re-united force to the governor's house which is where the gold and silver were stored prior to shipment to Spain. The Spanish were by now realising what a tiny force had attacked the town and were returning and re-grouping when a violent thunderstorm struck. The rain soaked the powder and bowstrings of Drake's men who started to lose heart and talked of leaving. Drake, wounded

Crowndale House, near Tavistock, accepted as Drake's birthplace

Buckland Abbey, Drake's home

and in pain, made a typical and rallying remark. "I have brought you to the treasure house of the world. If you leave without it you may henceforth blame no-one but yourselves". Drake's rallying call worked but was to prove worthless, because when they broke into the treasure house they found it empty, the Spanish fleet having sailed some weeks before taking the treasure with them. The next treasure deliveries from Panama would not start for several months until the next collection fleet arrived.

The raid had been a complete failure and Drake, bleeding badly from his leg wound, was carried to the pinnaces and away from Nombre de Dios. Captain Raunse decided to leave the expedition. He had prizes of his own and the Spanish were now fully alerted to their presence so a return to England was timely.

From his Cimarroon allies Drake learned when the next mule train carrying gold and silver would leave Panama for the port of Venta Cruces and he decided to wait for it. He filled in the time making raids along the coast and exploring the hinterland. On 11th February 1573 his Cimarroon friends took him to the top of a ridge from which he got his first look at the Pacific Ocean. During this time he lost both of his brothers, John and Joseph. John died from wounds received in a raid against the Spanish, and Joseph from yellow fever which had taken a high toll among Drake's men.

Planned raids on mule trains carrying gold, silver and silks failed, but his luck turned when he met a French privateer called Guillaume le Tetu. The Frenchman told Drake of another mule train carrying silver which was heading for Nombre de Dios. The 190 mules each carried 300 pounds of silver. The combined force of Drake and le Tetu successfully took the mule train and at last the expedition was in profit. The financial success of the raid was exactly what Drake needed to restore the morale of his men after months of fighting on land and sea, but le Tetu and several others lost their lives in the action.

The treasure captured from the mule train and the spoils from their previous activities amounted to some fifteen tons of silver ingots and approximately £100,000 value in gold coins. The expedition was now a success, and Drake decided to return home. The *Swan* had been scuttled and the *Pascoe* was not thought fit for the homeward Atlantic crossing so Drake captured a Spanish ship. It was aboard this vessel that Drake, his men and their treasure arrived back in Plymouth in April 1573. A possible slant on Drake's character is that one report indicates he cheated his brother John's widow out of her share of the proceeds of the expedition!

During this campaign John Oxenham had accompanied Drake when he crossed the Isthmus of Panama and glimpsed the Pacific Ocean. During the next few years Drake served the Crown mostly in European waters, and in 1576 John Oxenham set sail again for the Spanish Main to capitalise on the knowledge gained while serving under Drake. Oxenham's expedition proved ill-fated, but as they had on the previous Drake expedition they took pinnaces with them to re-assemble and use for shallow water work. On reaching the Spanish Main Oxenham crossed the Panama Isthmus, and in a pinnace became the first English captain to sail the Pacific Ocean. This considerable achievement has been largely forgotten and ignored by history.

The venture ended with the entire crew being captured by the Spanish and hanged as pirates. Oxenham was not executed with his men but met his fate later after having been taken to Lima for interrogation.

Drake was not a pirate of the same type as Blackbeard, Henry Avery or Bartholomew Roberts, but the Spanish referred to him as a pirate, and although he was acting in the name of Queen Elizabeth and was flying the flag of St George, there is no doubt that many of his acts of plunder and looting were piracy.

The incident of Spanish treachery - when they reneged on the deal and attacked Drake and Hawkins several years earlier - had left a lifelong mark on Drake. Just as Nelson had the French as his lifelong enemy, Drake had the Spanish. He was respected by his men, a good tactician, an adventurer by nature, and was bold and decisive. Attacking the Spanish made him a rich man and the Queen and other financial backers all profited from his expeditions.

On 13th December 1577 Drake, aboard the *Golden Hind*, led a small fleet of four other ships out of Plymouth on what would be a two year voyage involving a circumnavigation of the globe. Loss of ships, men and sedition beset the enterprise from the outset. Drake's one time friend Thomas Doughty was mutinous and was tried by Drake and some of his officers while they refitted at Port St. Julian near the Strait of Magellan. Doughty was found guilty and executed, which served to underline Drake's authority and deter others. In September 1578 three ships entered the Pacific Ocean and ran straight into a major storm during which the *Marigold* was lost and the *Golden Hind* and *Elizabeth* blown south. Soon after turning north again they were hit by another storm which separated the two ships. They did not manage to re-make contact and Captain Winter commanding the *Elizabeth* returned to England.

Drake pressed on, cruising north along the coast of Chile raiding Spanish shipping and shore settlements as he went. The treasure ship *Nuesta Senora de la Concepcion* was nicknamed *Cacafuego* which meant shitfire, and Drake decided to take her using an old pirate trick of altering the appearance of his own boat to trick his victim into a sense of false security and gain the advantage of surprise. The trick worked and captain San Juan de Anton was completely fooled. Drake boarded the treasure ship and took her captain and company prisoner. An inspection of the contents of the *Cacafuego's* hold confirmed that Drake had secured a rich prize. Thirteen chests of plate, 80 lbs of gold and 26 tons of silver were registered in various names including the King of Spain, and in addition there was unregistered treasure amounting to a slightly larger value. The captain valued the whole haul at 762,000 pesos which would be over £15 million today.

Drake was generous to Captain San Juan and released him and his crew with letters of safe conduct and gifts. This generosity did nothing to assuage the rage of the Spanish who set about trying to find and capture him in earnest. The way south and back home through the Strait of Magellan was effectively blocked by the Spanish, so Drake turned north. He found the way apparently blocked by land and turned south and spent a month anchored in the vicinity of what is now San Francisco. With the south route option closed by the Spanish and the north blocked by land he had to go west and in July 1579 set out across the Pacific. They sailed past the Philippines, the Moluccas (Spice islands), survived grounding on a reef in Indonesia, and in mid-June sailed around the Cape of Good Hope. They stopped to take on stores in Sierra Leone and reached Plymouth on 26th September 1580.

This two year and nine month epic voyage made Drake the first commander to circumnavigate the globe. Magellan's ship was the first but Magellan had been killed in the Philippines and so did not complete the whole voyage himself. The enormous value of Drake's captured treasure more than made up for any embarrassment Queen Elizabeth might have felt due to Drake's plundering of the Spanish. She was a major investor in the enterprise and reaped a handsome return. To the English he was a national hero and the Queen knighted him, to the Spanish he was 'a vile pirate' and the Ambassador complained of his actions and demanded compensation. The Queen authorised Drake to keep £10,000 for himself and £8,000 for his men, and while estimates of the value of the treasure vary it is likely that in today's terms Drake brought home £70/£80 million in precious stones, metals and other valuables. Drake's 'piracy' caused a sharp deterioration in the relationship between England and Spain and in 1585 war was declared between the two countries. Attacking the Spanish for plunder and treasure

Bust of Sir Francis Drake in Buckland Abbey

was now legal and several other captains and adventurers made fortunes following Drake's example.

Pirate to the Spanish, hero to the English, in 1588 Drake helped destroy the Spanish Armada. Although even when holding a commission and in command of thirty ships against the Armada, he had an eye for profit as he chased and caught a Spanish payship called the *Rosario*, took her valuables and ransomed her officers. In 1596 he sailed to the Spanish Main for the last time. Drake contracted a fever, died, and was buried at sea. Pirate or hero depends on perspective, but beyond question is that Drake was an outstanding seafarer, commander, adventurer, and patriot. One of Devon's finest sons.

Chapter Three

North African (Barbary) Pirates

There are two connections between North Africa's infamous Barbary pirates and Devon and Cornwall. The two counties supplied men who taught the North Africans how to build ocean going ships and who joined them in plying their pirate trade, and later Devon and Cornwall became hunting grounds for north African pirates.

England's war with Spain provided employment for many of Devon and Cornwall's pirates. Of the ships that fought the Spanish Armada in 1588, only thirty-four of the 226 total belonged to the Royal Navy. Most of the English fleet were privateers who sailed as much for personal gain as they did for Queen and country. In 1603 King James succeeded Elizabeth and in 1604 he made peace with Spain. I think it's fair to say that James was not a popular or respected King among the adventurous sea dogs that had had such a good run against the Spanish during Elizabeth's reign. In their eyes he was a Scottish king who hated war, and having made peace with Spain the letters of marque which authorised privateers to attack England's enemies were no longer valid. The early seventeenth century found many pirates unemployed.

The Mediterranean was part of one of the routes from the East to Europe. Spices, silks and other luxuries were carried overland, loaded in Levantine ports and shipped across the Mediterranean to Europe. Pirates from North Africa's Barbary coast had raided across this rich hunting ground for centuries. These pirates had largely remained inside the Mediterranean because their ships were not really designed for open ocean and northern waters. Ocean going sailing ships replaced galleons rowed by slaves, and it was renegades from northern Europe who taught the Barbary pirates how to build the ships they needed for operations outside the Mediterranean.

John Ward stole a ship in Portsmouth and sailed for Tunis where he joined Tunisian pirates. Plymouth born William Bishop was an associate of Ward's and it is likely that either or both of them instructed the Tunisians in the art of building ocean going sailing vessels.

Little is known of Bishop's early career but he would almost certainly have been involved with the privateers of Elizabeth's reign. By 1607/1608 Bishop and Ward were teamed up with Anthony Johnson, and later Johnson and Bishop became partners without Ward being involved. They worked closely with Tunisian pirates who gave them vessels and supplies, but always held one of them hostage against the others return. By mid 1608 Bishop seems to have become a more independent operator as he had acquired his own ship and a largely European crew. Bishop's old associate John Ward was the acknowledged senior figure among the pirate gangs.

Captain Henry Pepwell of the Royal Navy was keen to destroy, or at least limit the activities of the Barbary pirates, and sought to capture or kill John Ward. He tried to recruit Bishop to help bring this about and Bishop agreed. However in a direct confrontation Bishop had neither the men nor the ships to be able to take on Ward, and so the plot came to nothing and Bishop resumed his career as a Barbary pirate.

A fleet of eleven pirate ships off west Ireland in August 1609 elected Bishop as their admiral, so he had clearly become a figure who commanded respect. However it appears he must have been recruited by the Crown as some sort of negotiator or go between, because in 1610 he was pardoned and started actively to negotiate terms for the surrender of other pirates.

———

The other side of the Barbary pirate relationship with Devon and Cornwall was Barbary raids against coastal settlements in both counties, the irony here is that these raids were only possible due to the ocean going vessels which had been built with the help of the westcountry men. Barbary raids were largely motivated by capturing people for sale in the slave markets. Fair white women were particularly prized but men were captured as well. By the mid-1620s raids were common and in 1625 Barbary pirates captured Lundy

Island. They used Lundy as a base for several weeks as they raided all along the coasts of north Devon and Cornwall from Ilfracombe to Padstow. Lundy is an excellent place from which to catch shipping moving in and out of the Bristol Channel, and the merchants in Bristol and the government were seriously concerned at the presence on Lundy of the foreign pirates. Lundy on the north coast wasn't the only area of Barbary activity, they snatched ships in Plymouth Sound, took sixty captives from a church in Mounts Bay, and it is generally accepted that in total around 1000 people were taken by Barbary pirates from Devon and Cornwall in 1625. In a ten-day period in 1626 the small south Cornish fishing port of Looe lost eighty people.

In 1631 seven pirates from Morocco were tried for piracy in the Admiralty Court of Devon and found guilty. Curiously, one of the Barbary pirates was actually a Devon man from Dartmouth called Thomas Norton. Norton himself had been captured in 1620 and sold in an Algiers slave market. He escaped and joined the pirates as a ship's carpenter. He was able to amass a small fortune and bought his freedom. He stayed with the pirates and became captain of a pirate ship, but when he later returned to his native Dartmouth he was recognised and denounced. This led to his arrest and trial with the other Barbary men.

Chapter Four

Stuart Times

While many of the Tudor pirates went to Newfoundland and the Barbary coast, there were others who stayed at home and continued their trade. Many Westcountry, Welsh, and Irish coastal communities were only too happy to trade with the pirates and provide bases, food, ammunition and equipment.

Thomas Salkeld, Peter Easton, John Nutt, Robert Nutt and others were all successful Westcountry pirates of this period. Salkeld had been a privateer during Elizabeth's reign and was probably an associate of William Bishop (see Chapter 3). When Bishop's pirate command fragmented after he received his pardon, Salkeld went his own way and in March 1610, together with sixteen men, captured Lundy Island and declared himself its king. His captives were set to work on the island as slaves and Salkeld's will was enforced by hanging those who did not obey him.

For the third time Lundy was a pirate stronghold and this time had its own king! Clearly Salkeld presented a threat to shipping in the Bristol Channel and Bristol's merchants were particularly concerned. Sir William Manson was dispatched to Bristol to fit out the 34 gun HMS *Assurance* and sail to Lundy to end Salkeld's reign and treachery. The *Assurance* was by no means ready so Manson proceeded to Lundy with a smaller vessel and only twenty-five men. Before Manson could reach the island there had been a revolt against Salkeld led by a man named George Escott. Salkeld and his men had left Lundy and thus eluded Manson, and George Escott was granted a pardon.

Word was put out to all the coastal settlements on both sides of the Bristol

Channel to look out for and report Salkeld, and Manson patrolled the channel looking for him.   However it was later learned that after leaving Lundy Salkeld had fallen in with another pirate, Peter Easton, and that Easton had thrown Salkeld overboard following a quarrel. Salkeld had been a colourful character and it's a shame we don't know more about him.

In 1602 at the end of Elizabeth's reign, Easton was hired to command three ships and sail for Newfoundland to protect the English fishing fleet operating there. Quite how he got on as the guardian of the fishing fleet is not clear. However after James I made peace with Spain, Easton together with many other Elizabethan privateers, turned his hand to piracy. There are records from 1607 of Easton working with Richard Robinson who was a Plymouth pirate, and in 1608 he was involved in an action against the Royal Navy's HMS *Tramontana*.

In Chapter 3 we saw how, in 1609, Plymouth-born William Bishop commanded a pirate fleet of eleven ships in the Irish Sea. In 1610, when Bishop was pardoned, his command passed to his Vice Admiral Peter Easton. In late 1610 Easton also made moves to gain a pardon for himself and his men by making proposals to the English government's representatives in Ireland. A temporary amnesty of forty days was declared and Easton waited for the results of his pardon application while having to observe various conditions.

At this time a small squadron of Dutch ships attacked and tried to seize Bishop and his vessel. This may have been in retaliation for an earlier act of piracy Bishop had committed against them. Easton used this attack as an excuse to deploy his squadron of nine ships in the channel. He said that his nine ships was not a large enough force to engage the Dutch so he seized two merchantmen in the channel and added them to his command.   Many thought this was just an excuse for an act of piracy and the story got even more confused as Easton claimed that some sailors from one of the seized vessels had tried to murder him. Easton and his men killed three or four of the alleged culprits and put the crews of both merchantmen together on one ship and let her go. Easton kept the larger of the two vessels, the *Concord*, and sailed back to Ireland to wait for the results of his pardon.

Easton's old friend William Bishop got involved in the negotiations, which resulted in Easton handing over the *Concord* and her cargo. A general pardon was issued to Easton and his men but they didn't hear of it until the deadline had passed. Fearing reprisals from the Royal Navy and the Dutch Navy the pirates split into three groups and fled. Easton together with fellow pirate captains Hewes and Harvey, sailed for Newfoundland where he finally got to hear of his pardon.

He ignored his pardon and continued in the ways of piracy. He captured Sir Roger Whitbourne who was a senior official with the Royal Authority and held him for nearly three months. Whitbourne persuaded Easton to seek another pardon to which Easton agreed and dispatched Captain Harvey to England to open talks. Although this pardon was issued very quickly it was preceded by a pardon issued by the Duke of Savoy. Easton and four ships with 900 men aboard sailed into the Mediterranean and to the port of Villafanca.

By 1615 Easton was in the Duke's Army in which he served with great success. This led to his being granted a substantial pension, being given the title of Marquis, converting to Catholicism and marrying into the Savoyard aristocracy. He spent the rest of his life there living in luxury as a nobleman until his death in 1620.

Stories of Easton are many and separating fact from fiction is impossible. What is certain however is that he was a very colourful character and whereas piracy led many to the gallows, it led Easton to riches and to joining Europe's nobility.

———————

The other Westcountry Stuart pirates of note were the Nutt brothers, John and Robert. They both managed long and successful pirate careers and their fates are not known for sure. John Nutt's career began as an employee of Sir George Calvert for whom he worked in Newfoundland waters protecting the English colony being established there. It didn't take him long to gather together a band of rogues, seize a French ship, and begin his career as a pirate. During a two-year period he added an English and a Flemish ship to his command and amassed a considerable fortune through piracy. By early 1623 his ship was back in English waters ferrying seamen to Newfoundland to escape the Royal Naval press gangs. Enabling folk to elude the press gangs made him something of a local hero in South Devon where he enjoyed widespread support among coastal people. His base was in Torbay where he had a wife and children and from this secure base he was able to venture forth and raid shipping at will.

While popular with the people, Nutt was becoming a highly wanted man by the authorities. There was little point in being rich and popular if you were living under the threat of the gallows, so Nutt started to make moves to try and secure a pardon. The maritime affairs of Devon and Cornwall were largely overseen by the Vice Admiral of Devon, Sir John Eliot. It had been Eliot's press gangs that Nutt had helped sailors elude by shipping them to Newfoundland. Sir John was the man with whom John Nutt would have to negotiate his pardon, and Sir John had by now received orders to arrest Nutt and his men. Whether Eliot was wary of Nutt's popularity and his strength in men and ships, or whether he just decided it was easier we will never know, but he essentially tricked Nutt by convincing him that he was already in possession of a pardon for him. While these initial pardon moves had been going on Nutt had not totally given up piracy and had seized a Colchester ship the *Edward and John* together with it's crew and a valuable cargo.

On the 6th June 1623, although Sir John Eliot had not yet received Nutt's pardon, he spent the whole day aboard Nutt's ship anchored in Torbay negotiating terms. Nutt agreed to pay a fine of £500 and six packs of calf skins. Soon after, when Nutt sailed into Dartmouth thinking he had secured his pardon, he and his men were arrested.

Prior to Nutt's arrest the Admiralty had ordered Eliot to ensure the return of the *Edward and John* to her owners. He had refused to take action, and now following Nutt's arrest the owners of the *Edward and John* claimed that Eliot had taken some of her cargo and he was arrested. For a man in Sir John Eliot's position to be arrested without proof was extraordinary, but his earlier refusal to obey Admiralty orders, and his tricking of the popular John Nutt, had not made him many friends.

The arrests and investigations of Nutt and Eliot are clouded by claim and counterclaim and little could be proved either in terms of guilt or innocence. Eliot was generally acknowledged as being innocent and Nutt as a pirate and a rogue. Nutt had a powerful friend at court in the shape of his one time employer Sir George Calvert who was now a Secretary of State and who wrote to the King on Nutt's behalf. Calvert argued that Nutt had been pardoned before and it was not his fault that he had not received the actual pardon. Nutt was pardoned again on the 18th of August 1623. Sir John Eliot's lack of friends at court and in the system counted against him and he was not released until November. Eliot languished in jail for three months after Nutt's release which must have been a bitter pill to swallow.

In 1627 Nutt is on record as having taken command of the privateer *Mary Margaret*. Later in 1627 there is record of John Nutt's brother Robert being in command of another privateer The *Mary*. Robert was clearly starting on the same pirate road that his brother was supposed to have given up when he was pardoned, as later in 1627 he seized a small London vessel the *Elizabeth* and sailed with her into Dartmouth harbour. The Admiralty Court declared the act as piratical but no case was bought against Robert who was instructed to return the vessel to its owners.

Both John and Robert Nutt commanded privateers and had letters of marque, (see page 56) and were active at sea using their letters to capture Dutch and Portuguese prizes. By 1631 Robert Nutt was in league with Jonathan Downes who was another privateer captain and together they sailed the Irish Sea, the English Channel and its approaches. Robert Nutt had found new colleagues by early 1632 and was sailing in consort with pirate captains Norman and Smyth both commanding privateers.In March 1632 Robert Nutt was pardoned by the King but confusingly, at the same time, instructions were issued for him to be apprehended. It may be that the order for his arrest or surrender were part of the terms of his pardon in that he was expected to give himself up within a certain time. Ironically one of the captains given responsibility for Robert Nutt's arrest was his brother John, the other was Thomas Kettleby of the Royal Navy.

John Nutt went to sea looking for his brother to give him his pardon. It appears that John never caught up with Robert, and by July of 1632 he was reported off the coast of Spain. There are then various reports of Robert off Britain's west coast and in late August he was nearly taken by Captain Plumleigh of the HMS *Assurance*. Plumleigh found Nutt off Scotland's west coast and Nutt mistook the *Assurance* for a merchantman and made the nearly fatal mistake of approaching her with the intention of boarding the naval vessel. Nutt realised his error in time and fled with his consort vessel while being fired at by the *Assurance*. Nutt's superior speed ensured his escape.

Plumleigh reported the incident and requested that the *Assurance* be joined by faster ships – he did not want Nutt to outrun him to freedom again. Nutt also made preparations and joined forces with a group of Barbary pirates operating in the Irish Sea. By the time they met again in October Plumleigh had two small faster ships as well as the *Assurance,* and Nutt and his allies were a fleet of nearly thirty ships. This time it was Plumleigh who had to flee and he made a lucky escape keeping all his ships afloat and intact.

Robert Nutt realised that having openly challenged the Royal Navy there was no way he could remain in British waters and so he sailed south across the Bay of Biscay to Spain. He did not have many options because having plundered and captured ships from many nations he had nowhere he could safely run to.

In November 1632 reports reached England that he had been captured by the Spanish and hanged at Corunna. However that may not have been the end of the Robert Nutt story because in 1636 bad weather drove a Spanish supply ship into Falmouth harbour. Aboard the Spanish vessel were a Robert

Nutt, Stephen Willing and John Billing. Willing and Billing had both been members of Nutt's crew so clearly the three had somehow evaded the hangman. They were all arrested but there is no confirmed record of what happened to them.

Whilst Robert continued to pursue his career as a pirate, his brother John stayed inside the law, captaining various privateers. The Nutt brothers were a colourful pair who had long and successful pirate careers and both probably died natural deaths.

Chapter Five

The English Civil War

In August 1642 the differences between King Charles I and his parliament, which had been building up for some time, came to a head and the Civil War started. Most of rural Devon and Cornwall were on the side of the King but many of the administrative and trading centres declared for Parliament. Plymouth, Exeter, Dartmouth and Barnstaple were Parliamentarian strong-holds surrounded by hostile Royalist hinterlands.

At the beginning things went well for the King's men who took all the Parliamentarian strongholds except Plymouth, to which they laid siege. The Royal Navy had taken the side of Parliament, and in the first part of the war the King's navy consisted of a mixed bag of privateers and pirates led by Admiral Sir John Pennington. The King didn't actually possess the power to grant licences to privateers, this was in the gift of the Lord Admiral who was on the Parliamentarian side. Therefore as far as Parliament was concerned the privateers working in the King's service were pirates.

Two of the most notable privateers sailing in the King's service were Captains Jones and Polhill who became adept at ambushing unsuspecting merchantmen. The Royal Navy sent two ships after Jones and Polhill and a battle occurred off the French coast. Polhill's ship the *Mayflower* surrendered, but when she was boarded it was discovered that Polhill had escaped earlier through a gun port. Little more is recorded about Jones, but Polhill continued in the service of the King and commanded other privateers.

When Dartmouth fell to the Royalists in October 1643 several new ships were added to those already in the King's service. By December 1643 the Earl of Malborough had command of a large number of ships in Dartmouth. Marlborough planned to sail to the Canaries, Madeira, the Azores and the Cape Verde islands and press all the English ships that he found into the King's service. The fleet would then continue on to New England and Newfoundland, adding to their numbers at every opportunity.

The Parliamentarians realised that were this plan to succeed the Royalists would have naval supremacy, so a Naval captain called Jordan with six ships was sent after Marlborough to stop him crossing the Atlantic. They played cat and mouse around the Channel Islands before Jordan gave up the chase and Marlborough returned to Dartmouth.

Oliver Cromwell's New Model Army was winning the war on land and Marlborough's plans to create a large naval fleet for the King came to nothing. By the end of the Civil War the only privateers operating in the King's name were a small squadron led by Prince Rupert, the King's nephew. From 1649 until 1660 the Protectorates of Oliver and Richard Cromwell replaced the monarchy, and in 1660 the House of Stuart was restored and Charles II ascended to the throne.

King Charles I

Oliver Cromwell

Chapter Six

An Extraordinary Character

William Dampier was born the son of a farmer at East Coker, Somerset, in 1652. While technically not a pirate of Devon and Cornwall he was far too interesting a character to leave out of this book because of having been born in a next-door county. Dampier was an author, a diarist, buccaneer, sea captain, naturalist, and one of the great navigators of his time. His life and those with whom he associated is worth examination.

Dampier's parents died while he was a child and so he was brought up by guardians. In 1669 at seventeen years old his guardians sent him to sea, having secured him a job on a Weymouth ship bound for Newfoundland. His next voyage was to the East Indies before he joined the Royal Navy in 1673. He was aboard the *Royal Prince*, which was Sir Edward Spragge's flagship for the two battles of Schoonveld against the Dutch. He was ill and in the sick bay for the battle of the Texel in which Sir Edward Spragge was killed. Invalided out of the Navy he went home to Somerset to stay with his brother while recovering. One of his neighbours was Colonel Hellier who owned plantations in Jamaica and who offered Dampier a job as an assistant manager on a plantation.

He left England in 1674 working his passage to Jamaica. His first job lasted about six months and then he was offered a job managing another plantation for a Captain Hemming. He soon tired of plantation work and was back at sea engaged in the logwood trade. This was a highly lucrative business and one ton of wood was worth £5 - £10 when sold to local merchants and then was worth around £100 a ton in England. He returned to England in 1678 and

William Dampier

married a member of the household staff of the Duchess of Arlington called Judith. The new Mrs Dampier saw her husband for just over six months before he was off to sea again where he spent most of the next ten years.

In 1679 he joined the buccaneer band led by Captain Bartholemew Sharpe. They sailed first to Portobello and captured and ransacked the city. Next their ambitions led them to try an attack on Panama City. By the time they had marched across the isthmus to the city there were eight Spanish men of war lying at anchor. They captured a small ship and a number of canoes and while Sharpe was off chasing another ship the remainder of the buccaneers led by a Captain Coxon decided to attack the ships from their canoes. Despite heavy losses Coxon's men amazingly captured five of the Spanish ships. The heavy losses meant abandoning plans to attack the city and the pirates withdrew and split into two groups. One group elected to stay and the other, which was Dampier's group and which was led by Captain John Cook, retraced their steps back to the Caribbean coast.

August 1683 found Dampier and Cook in Virginia planning another adventure to the Pacific. They sailed aboard the *Revenge* for West Africa and here they took a large forty gun Dutch vessel which suited them better and which they re-named the *Bachelors Delight*. Further down the coast they exchanged the *Revenge* for sixty black girls and then set sail for Cape Horn. Many seamen of the day were very superstitious and it was widely believed that having women on board brought bad luck. In mid February 1684 near Cape Horn the *Bachelors Delight* was caught in a terrible storm which blew them south. They reached sixty degrees and thirty minutes south which was thought to be the furthest south that any vessel had reached.

A change of wind in early March enabled them to enter the Pacific at last where they met up with Captain John Eaton of the *Nicholas* who had survived the same storm. The *Nicholas* and the *Bachelors Delight* sailed together for Juan Fernandez where an extraordinary surprise awaited them. Three years earlier Dampier and his fellow buccaneers had been on Juan Fernandez when the arrival of three Spanish ships had caused them to flee. Such was the haste of their escape that they left one of their company behind by mistake. William was a Mosquito Indian and he had survived, Robinson Crusoe fashion, on the island. William had survived well and he cooked a feast to welcome the return of his old shipmates.

From Juan Fernandez they set out northwards for the area of Panama where they hoped to ambush the Spanish treasure fleet on its way up the coast. The fleet did not materialise and a plan for another attack on Panama City was abandoned. The presence of several English buccaneers in the region had made the Spanish very cautious, and they had fortified many of their settlements and were not going to provide any easy pickings.

Dampier's band decided to sail for the Galapagos to lie low and repair and re-supply their ships. One of his interests was nature and the Galapagos offered him many opportunities to study flora and fauna in that extraordinary environment. Dampier made copious notes and recorded everything he came across. One of his shipmates called Cowley gave many of the islands the names they still have to this day – King Charles Island, York, Norfolk, and Alblemarle, were named after the monarch and his dukes while Brattle, Crossman, Euyre, and Bandloss were named after other members of the pirate band. Cowley named one small island after himself – Cowley's Island. In September 1684 the *Nicholas* and the *Bachelors Delight* parted company after leaving the Galapagos and cruising for prizes with no success.

A few weeks later the *Bachelors Delight* met two other buccaneer vessels one of which was called the *Cygnet* and was appropriately skippered by a Captain Swan! The combined force again set their sights on Panama, but again the presence of a large Spanish squadron prevented a successful attack.

Dissent was rife and eventually Dampier threw in his lot with Captain Swan and after more months of unsuccessful operations they set sail in March 1686 across the Pacific in two vessels bound for the East Indies. It took fifty one days to reach the island of Guam and a shortage of food was one of the continual worries. Apparently the men had decided that those who had proposed the journey across the Pacific would be to blame if supplies ran out, and they would be killed and eaten should the desperate need arise. They reached Guam with only three days food left and so Dampier and Captain Swan avoided being eaten. Swan was a large fat man and Dampier as thin as a rake, and Swan is supposed to have remarked to Dampier "you would have made them but a poor meal!".

After re-supplying at Guam they sailed on to the Philippines and spent some weeks at Mandingo where their men spent most of what they had earned in the bars and on prostitutes. Eventually there was a mutiny led by a Bristol man called John Reed. Swan and thirty of his men were left in Mandingo when Reed, Dampier and the other buccaneers sailed away. For most of 1687 they cruised the Spice Islands, the Indian Ocean and landed in Australia. In May 1688 Dampier left the buccaneers and spent the next two years on various trading expeditions in the Indian Ocean. He arrived back in England on an East India Company convoy in 1691.

Dampier had not been home or seen his wife for twelve years and arrived home broke with little to show for his travels except his copious notes. He was a great diarist and in 1697 published a book called 'A New Voyage Around the World'. The book was, and indeed still is, a great success and has delighted readers for over three centuries. Dampier was a contemporary of that other great diarist Samuel Pepys and it is said they knew each other. The book not only records the voyages and the exploits of the pirates, it also has wonderful descriptions of strange new lands, native peoples and new birds and animals. He reproduced several pages from his logbooks and showed how he made his course calculations.

In 1699 he was given the command of the Royal Naval ship the *Roebuck* and sailed for Australia in January. The *Roebuck* was a small naval vessel of 290 tonnes and she had five long guns. On the return voyage she sprang a leak near Ascension Island and Dampier abandoned her to sink. He and his crew made it ashore in a raft and were picked up some weeks later by a squadron of British warships. On his return to England Dampier was declared unfit to command a naval vessel and was court martialled.

However, in 1703 he was selected to command a privately financed expedition to the Pacific. He had two ships which were to operate as privateers to secure a profitable return for the merchants who backed the venture. The expedition was ill fated from the start and the two ships didn't even manage to sail together because Dampier delayed his departure waiting for one of his key men to be released from prison. He sailed to Kinsale in southern Ireland in April, spent the summer refitting and provisioning, and eventually in September set off in company with another ship the *Cinque Ports*.

Dampier did not return until autumn 1707 having spent four years operating as a privateer with no real financial success. In fact one of his associates had stolen his letters of marque, so when in the Dutch East Indies he was required to show them to prove he was not a pirate, he couldn't and he and his crew were thrown in jail.

A remarkable feature of this expedition was that the sailing master of the *Cinque Ports*, Alexander Selkirk, decided, near Juan Fernandez, that the ship was un-seaworthy. He refused to sail in her and marooned himself when the ship left. He expected Dampier to come to the island but this didn't happen and he was marooned for four years and four months until he was found in 1709 by another expedition with Dampier aboard. Selkirk's story was later published and inspired Daniel Defoe to write Robinson Crusoe.

Dampier's second book 'A Voyage to New Holland' was published in 1709 and described the disastrous *Roebuck* expedition. His return to England in 1707 marked the completion of his second circumnavigation. What had happened on the four year voyage, who was responsible for the mistakes, and the expedition's lack of financial success, were hotly debated.

In 1708 another expedition was financed by merchants and Captain Woodes Rogers of Bristol was given command. Woodes Rogers recognised the huge value of Dampier's unequalled knowledge of the South Seas and took him on as pilot for the venture. Unlike previous expeditions in which Dampier had been involved, this one which lasted from 1708 until 1711 was a huge financial success. Many rich prizes were taken and the investors and crews reaped a good profit. When the ships dropped anchor in the Thames in October 1711 Dampier had returned from his third circumnavigation. William Dampier died in 1715, he was certainly one of the leading sailors of his age and rarely gets the recognition he deserves.

Chapter Seven

Avery, Gulliford and Condent

Henry Avery (Every) was born in Plymouth in 1653 and was the son of innkeeper John Avery. Avery was a typical pirate who had books and plays written about him, such as 'The Successful Pirate' which ran for several years at the Drury Lane Theatre. The Daniel Defoe book 'The King of the Pirates' was based on his discussions with Avery. Archetypal pirate he may have been but he was probably not the slim, attractive and athletic Captain Jack Sparrow type! Some reports have him as being of average height, rather fat, with a dissolute appearance and a ruddy complexion; however, one of his nicknames was Long Ben which was a way of describing someone who was taller than average. This contradiction is a good example of the difficulties faced by researchers trying to get at the facts!

Avery's life at sea started in the Royal Navy in which he served aboard HMS *Rupert* and HMS *Albemarle* as a midshipman. In 1694 he was second mate aboard a Bristol privateer the *Charles the Second* which sailed for Corunna on her way to raid the Spanish colonies.

The ship spent several months in Corunna with the crew getting more restless each day. Eventually on May 7th there was a mutiny led by Avery while the Captain lay drunk in his cabin. Avery announced "I am captain of this ship now. I am bound for Madagascar with the design of making my fortune, and that of all the brave fellows joined with me". The pirates renamed their ship the *Fancy* and sailed south. At the Cape Verde Islands they took three English ships, and then at the island of Principe they added two Danish ships to their small fleet.

After rounding the Cape of Good Hope he made for Madagascar, where they dropped anchor, and set about re-supplying. Avery's plan was to go to the mouth of the Red Sea, and wait there to intercept ships of the Pilgrim fleet which sailed each year from the Indian port of Surat to Mocha. The pilgrim ships were an attractive prospect for pirates as they often carried valuable spices which could be traded for silver and gold. Avery sailed from Madagascar with the *Fancy*, *Pearl*, and *Portsmouth Adventure* and was joined at sea by the *Vanity* commanded by another famous pirate, Thomas Tew. The number of guns aboard the *Fancy* had been increased to 46 in Madagascar and her crew numbered 150 men. With a powerful ship of his own augmented by three others Avery lay in wait hoping for rich prizes. Somehow much of the Pilgrim fleet slipped past Avery unnoticed, but eventually a large Indian ship the *Fatah Mohammad* came into view and was taken by the pirates. She was looted of gold and silver worth over £50,000 but Thomas Tew was killed in the fight to take her.

A few days later Avery sighted a much larger ship which turned out to be the *Gang-I-Sawai*. This ship belonged to the Great Mogul and was armed with sixty-two guns and had four hundred rifles to defend against attack. The *Fancy* was, for a pirate ship, a potent fighting vessel but she was outgunned by the *Gang-I-Sawai* so Avery decided to stand off and pound her with his guns in the hope of disabling and boarding her. Lady luck was sailing with him as one of his first shots brought down the Indian ship's main mast. The lighter ships closed in and boarded her, and then the *Fancy* came up and Avery's men also swarmed aboard the Muslim ship. What followed can only be described as an orgy of looting, rape, and torture and certainly there was nothing romantic or chivalrous about the behaviour of the pirates. Avery denied that harm was done to the women aboard the *Gang-I-Sawai*. However at later pirate trials members of his crew admitted to horrible barbarities. The ships lay together becalmed for several days during which time the rape and looting continued.

The financial value of the haul was huge with gold, silver and jewels being the main items of value. Each man in Avery's command who was entitled to a full share received about £1000, which was nearly 60 years wages for an able seaman. Avery convinced the other captains that the loot would be safest aboard his ship the *Fancy* because she was the largest, most seaworthy, and best armed. They sailed together for a few days and then awoke one morning to find Avery and the *Fancy* gone, so their share of the loot had sailed away without them. The value of this single pirate act was one of the largest coups in pirate history, and Avery decided to retire while he was still rich and free.